DATE DUE

MAR 1 0 2010

shadow
box

shadow box

POEMS

Fred Chappell

LOUISIANA STATE UNIVERSITY PRESS

BATON ROUGE

Published by Louisiana State University Press
Copyright © 2009 by Fred Chappell
All rights reserved
Manufactured in the United States of America
First printing

Designer: Laura Roubique Gleason
Typefaces: Arno Pro (text), Centaur (display)
Printer and binder: Thomson-Shore, Inc.

Some of the poems herein first appeared in *Anglican Theological Review,
Appalachian Heritage, Cut Throat, Solo Café 2,* and *Turnrow,* and in
Kakalak: An Anthology of Carolina Poets, edited by Lisa Zerkle, Richard
Allen Taylor, and Beth Cagle Burt.
    "The Foreseeing" and "Searchlight" were published as separate
broadsides by Jerry Reddan at Tangram in Berkeley, California.
    "Narcissus and Echo" was first published in *Spring Garden: New and
Selected Poems* (Louisiana State University Press, 1995).
    Special thanks go, as always, to Porter Aichele and to Susan Nicholls
Chappell. When Job's patience ran dry, theirs still ran constant.

Library of Congress Cataloging-in-Publication Data

Chappell, Fred, 1936–
  Shadow box : poems / Fred Chappell.
    p. cm.
  ISBN 978-0-8071-3452-8 (alk. paper) — ISBN 978-0-8071-3453-5 (pbk. : alk.
paper)
  I. Title.
  PS3553.H298S53 2009
  811'.54—dc22
                        2008055653

for Mary von Schrader Jarrell

Contents

foreword

It is a wonderful testimonie of our judgments imbecilitie, that it should commend and allow things, either for their rareness or noveltie, or for their difficultie, though neither goodnesse or profit be joyned unto them.

> —Montaigne, *Essays,* bk. I, chap. LIV: "Of Vaine Subtlities, or Subtill Devices"

Part One

: in which poems-within-poems (*enclosed, inlaid, embedded, double, nested*) present two aspects of a situation or personality simultaneously. Each whole poem implies a narrative incomplete without these different perspectives. The points of view are distinguished by separate type faces.

In the poems taking place in a retirement home, the personalities may be caged within disabling mental conditions such as Alzheimer's disease.

Sometimes these poems, and others scattered throughout the volume, are curtal sonnets in which sestets are embedded in octaves.

The Foreseeing

If he could love her less, he might succeed in seeming unaware
of those fleet changes in her she herself would never recognize,
    not seeing how *her shadow that had bleached until* it was a bare
half-shadow, until *it was the color of morning rain,* seeing nowhere
        signal that it *will now begin to overfill* (the way that sighs
overfill breathing) *its edgeless contours with a serene* and depthless power,
        a resistless *immaculate azure like sky-shine:* and though he tries,
    deception fails *because she is in love again,* and mist-cold
fear he can no longer flee or put from him with well-intentioned lies
    comes on like April's heartless frost to wither him once more.

The Afterthought

Might it never have happened if he had not believed he had foreseen
the shabby shape of things to come? If he could read into her heart
with certainty, why *could he not disclose his mind* to her, impart
 his sawblade fear, *and tell what sorrow ravaged days* that stood between
the silent pair, *omitting all the impotent lies* he used to screen
himself from truth, *pretending no more to be blind* to what must part
them, indifferent *to facts that lay before his eyes*? To make a start,
he might hold her *and say he loved her, would always,* and she alone
was motive not to be insane, if he were not already insane,
confessing that he knew one blue day he would wake to find her gone.

Searchlight

The hamlet sleeps under November stars.
Only *the page of numerate thought* toils through
The darkness, *shines on the table where,* askew
And calm, *the scholar's lamp burns bright* and scars
The silence, *sending through the slot,* the bars
And angles *of his window square,* a true
Clean ray, *a shaft of patient light,* its purview
Lonely and remote as the glow of Mars.

Neverland

That time will not return that she has borne
So deeply in her mind. Together again
In the cozy bungalow on Paxton Street—
Forgetting then *what lies* they had exchanged,
Those weepy quarrels *across* the breakfast table—
They reunited in *her hopes* forever,
Although that house *these days* has lost all charm,
The yard weed-choked, and where *is that* porch swing
That once consoled *the loss* of summer days?
This is her dream *of what* a dream should be,
Vision of what *once was* that never was,
Where all that *could not* happen surely happened,
And all the things that *take place* never may.
From here they shall go on *without* each other,
Living two lives *her lies* cannot repair.
In some bright Other Time unreachable
From now they live on Paxton Street still young—
And under summer stars their yard lies clean.

If you wish hard enough, it must be true.

Stopping by the Old Homestead

The Interstate is audible from here.
Five miles east, its low, autonomous hum
disturbs *the stillness that then stood,* the calm
you found *when you came here last time,* eight years
ago, *climbing the same hard road* you toiled
in youth *that slants a steeper grade* today,
this path *by the twisted apple tree* whose shadow
tensely *holds a darker tone.* You breathe
harder *than when you stopped to see* this farm
back then, where *claims your life had made* against
the future *and never paid to own* decayed.
Old times *shriveled and largely gone,* you think,
and trudge all down the hill to find your Chevy
rust-eaten, blind, jacked up on cinder blocks.

Psychoanalysis

The soldiers devour the politic boundaries;
The maps expunge the accustomed names of nations.
No one can say *if the force of the storm* now sees
Its deadly future, *could ever discover* the motions
Of its being, *what dark motive force* inside
Its history *compels it over* again
And again to attack *calm city and farm,* to stride
In thunder, trying *to flee its source,* to reign
To ruin. We think *it might disarm,* disdain
To drown these innocent lives in innocent blood—
If it looked into itself and understood.

Serenity

The storm came tumbling from the yellow west
And flung upon Crabbe Cove and our drab houses.
The lightning speared an elm and then the steeple
Of the Holiness; *a rain* gust clubbed the eaves;
Darkness like curtain-*drop slid* down the sky
And the roaring made *its way* over the mountain
Past Tyler Knob and rolled *all down* the valley.
We stood secure behind *the pane,* we thought,
And crowded all *in one* dim room to gape.
Had all marched in the *straight line* of virtue?
We reassured ourselves *amid* the onslaught
We need not fear *the loud* bugling of wind,
The bewildered *affray* that took the place
Of Nature, fury *that tore* the tender weave
Of Mind to shreds, drowning *the world* and all
The world had meant, driving *apart* the men
And valiant women *with storm* outside the house,
With storm *inside* the room, so everywhere
That we were there *its heart* clenched and unclenched.
A little girl stood at the window, doll
In arms, to watch one drop glide down the glass,
Taking its own unhurried time, at last
Uncommonly to join the common rain.

The Caretakers

We tend the grave of the broken son of man.
We keep the silent house without a hearth
Wherein *the man with vacant stare* and gaptooth grin
Calmly *searches his gleamless night* of earth,
Aloof, *in sober, patient state* alone,
Bemused, *aware or unaware* of stone
That spells *his name and final date.* Again,
Fresh flowers *stand boldly in the light* cold rain
Amid the winds that scour down from the north.
We are the grass, the rain. We are the sun.

In the Retirement Home

1

The Old Revolutionary

He rolls his narrow life from day to day,
Denies *the youth that cruelty* had maimed,
Those years *once shaped to a contour* now disclaimed,
Decades *jagged with black rage* gone gray.
His mind *departs, setting him free* to stray
The halls, *to roam, like a minotaur,* unfamed
And mute, *the labyrinth of age,* ashamed:
"And that which once was great, is passed away."

2

One Yet Remembers

He understands she cannot call his name.
And now *the secret that explained* whatever
They had been, *the pact that made them one,* clever
And deadly, *and darkened her sly mind,* as flame
Is snuffed, *and all it had maintained,* the same.
That time *is now forever gone,* forever
Canceled, *leaving no trace behind,* though never
Will he forget their naked, devouring shame.

3

The Elder Poet's Search

Through tears she sees him fumble about the room
And how *from his troubled shelves he takes* this one
And that, *the volumes of friends long dead,* undone
Or done with, *and in their stanzas seeks* with numb
Fingers *lines that when first read* in gloom
Or joy *shone warm as island lakes* in sun.
She sees him, *now grown chill with dread,* write down
The granite words she must order for his tomb.

4

Round and Round

All things circle slow, then fast, then slow
Again. *The night nurse flutters by,* the bed,
The curtain, *a white and silent wraith* outspread,
The lamp *whose blind transcendent stare* burns low.
Her gaze *is fixed on things most high,* aglow
With rapture *beyond the wasting faith* that fed
The mind *of Mother in her wheelchair* with dread,
With nauseate, never-ending vertigo.

5

Past Presence

You lie in customary oblivion
until, *in its cloak of wind-flawed rain,* outside
the window *one midnight steps apart,* a stride
away *from its shrouded sibling hours,* alone
and dim, *to recall an ancient pain* and bemoan
your past *with all its brooding powers* denied.
And now *within your ravaged heart* there glide
time-eaten phantoms with cold eyes of stone.

6

Revenant

Cleaning her comb, she finds a remnant trace—
and sighs. *She lays this single hair,* this one
revenant *that gives the lie to truth,* a lone
survivor, *across the palm of her hand;* her gaze
transfixed *conjures in near despair* to erase
from mind *the glory that was Youth,* this sun-
shine thread, *the grandeur that was Blonde,* now done:
one golden strand among the thousand grays.

Black Gate

You go out when the midnight calls your name
Into a *silent and immense* wrong space.
The Gate, *that unreflective stone* your gaze
Avoids, *hingeless shall turn but once,* when time
Permits, *and when that shall be done,* shall claim
The egress, *refuse the least response,* and cease
To open *to woman, child, or man,* fix grace
On anything you did or path you came.

Empathy

Anywhere I walk this town my blood
Can feel *beneath the avenues* the veins
Through which *a nameless water bears* through mains
Of iron *the city's stinking poison* abroad.
I taste *the muddy ochres and blues* that flood
The earth *to the farthest sulfur shores,* where drains
Nourish *the glowing, stagnant ocean,* and rains
Corrode forever the passive, unstarred void.

Mirage

1

Somewhere sidewise lies the untitled time of earth
before the mind becomes a work of art, disposing
all it beholds to cities, groves, and gardens; *before
the heart becomes a work of mind* to order passion
into measured ranks and stations; *before that part
of what could never depart* eludes our sight but not
our vision; *before the lost world dies without a sound;*

there shine sweet pastures on the slopes of eternity.

2

Afterward, *the woman with unseeing eyes,*
having *told our fate as sour exile,* predicted
that we should bide under alien skies of iron
and spend long years in heartless toil under the gaze
of hungry fellow captives and murderous captors
while always that goodly ancient time now lost when we
were so well lodged *drew farther from our bitter track,*
beckoning us *into a delusive age to come,*
mirage, *some gold eon of unspoilable luck:*

a time when we were free to think that we were free.

3

Deceived by prophecy, *exiled by a promise
misunderstood,* we end our journey. *A meteorite
falling we took as guide* and followed its red arc
and where this cold star struck upon the land we settled.
Here *were leagues on heartsick leagues of savage sand.*

We hardly look at one another now, turning
away *for fear we might recall the time of grace*
we habited, *forever lost to us we know*
not how nor when nor wherefore and so we shall submit
one truth: *Our loss is written upon every face:*

a past that will not pass from mortal memory.

A Face in the Crowd

Those days she was no part
Of anything else he knew
Or thought of. She was she,
Woman who claimed his heart,
If she claimed one at all,
Woman he saw anew
Each time he saw her, free
Of everything that stood
Between them and beside,
Image that made of place
Mere setting. He never would
Forget that form, that face
Until the hour he died.

As when the streets are calm and a lone figure
stands waiting, or walks idly up and down,
isolate and prominent in the scene,
but then is lost to sight when stadium gates
loose to the city a moiling, red-faced crowd:
So these days flood those days she was no part
of anything else. He knew her then as Love,
distinct from others perceived or thought of. *She*
was *she*. There was a woman who claimed his heart
before they met, another—if she claimed one
at all—some long time after. There was a woman
he saw anew while their affair went on,
but then each time he saw her *she* stood free
of everything that could distract, of all
that stood between them and beside. Apart,
he saw her as in a candle-lighted niche,
image so loved it made of place mere setting.

Those days he vowed he never would forget.
That form, that face would haunt his deepest dreams,
and brightest, until the hour he died.
                                    The years
came onward still, bearing more dreams with faces
and forms nothing like hers, a vivid stream
that grew less vivid with the passing nights.
He married; he fathered children; he forgot;
then one day in the shopping mall he saw
the face of one he thought that he should know.

A Drop in the Bucket

Inside this bucket made of white oak staves
wherewith they carry water from the well,
I feel *I am the I I am,* contained
and whole, *because in this small space,* restrained
and still, *there is insufficient room* to move
about, *for places to change place,* to rove
at chance, *and the stiller things become* (the pail
set down) *the more am I the I I am* (oak leaves
falling around the cabin, cool stars streaming above).

A Drop in the Ocean

I hate the public but adore the people.
—Jack Chase

I do not know how I have come to be
this self within the waters of the planet.
I feel *I am a part of all* the sea,
body *from which I am not apart.* In it
I feel *I am a member of* the whole
motion, *something indivisible,* complete,
immense, *and whatever thing it is,* so great
in mass, *is not individual* of will.

Always *I move as it moves me,* today,
tonight *when the moon exerts its might* below
and throbs *with all its massive light* at play
full strength *on each atom of the sea.* I know
and do not know how I have come to be
so ill defined, an I that is not me.

Narcissus and Echo

Shall the water not remember   *Ember*
my hand's slow gesture, tracing above   *of*
its mirror my half-imaginary   *airy*
portrait? My only belonging   *longing,*
is my beauty, which I take   *ache*
away and then return as love   *of*
of teasing playfully the one being   *unbeing.*
whose gratitude I treasure   *Is your*
moves me. I live apart   *heart*
from myself, yet cannot   *not*
live apart. In the water's tone,   *stone?*
that shining silence, a flower   *Hour,*
whispers my name with such slight   *light,*
moment, it seems filament of air,   *fare*
the world become cloudswell.   *well.*

24

AWOL

The sonnet "Bolus" is missing from this book
for timorous reasons of propriety;
it recalled the perfidies and insolent shames,
deceptions, *evasions and outright lies* of one
whose cool *contemptuous attitude* we saw
as aimed *toward everything sound and good* prevailing
too long *in the purblind public eye.* At last
I canceled, *for reasons that would try* beyond
the limit *the keen insight of Freud,* those lines,
hoping *the charity of God,* forbearance
of Susan, *wisdom of the ages,* might prevail.
I'd write *and fill a thousand pages* with names
and facts no one would give a second look.
That's why "Bolus" is missing from this book.

[Intervention]

"Retain 'Bolus,' *I say,*" Susan told me.
A poet must *do right,* be ever free
To speak his piece *by day* with liberty
And speak again *at night* though none will see."

Bolus

"This pill is good for you," the President said.
"It sweats the body and it warms the head.
We take *old shredded documents* and add
Numbing *phrases without sense,* combine
With expensive *neo-imperial hubris,* refine
Our normal *self-satisfied b.s.,* knead in
A dram of *childish arrogance,* and blend
Ice-cold *stiff-necked petulance,* begin
A quack *invasion enterprise* we fed
With fear *compacted all of lies* and spread
Foot-thick with *unmitigated gall then* boiled
All down with *spirits of ideals fallen* spoiled.
It stiffens the prick and resurrects the dead.
This pill is good for you," the President said.

Part Two

: in which the poems center upon visual images. The inner italicized verses may emphasize details, as in film close-ups, while the complete poems provide wider vistas, as in long or medium-long shots.

Or vice versa.

Crossed Sticks

Don't Look Back, your early title advised,
An irony that our America
Believes implicitly. The country club,
Neon fast-food strip, tanning salon,
Emerge from seeming nowhere into time,
Young for an hour, frowsy in a day.

So soon our images effloresce and pass
That we who try to fix them to a point
Understand that San Pietro, Dachau,
Anzio, inconceivable Iwo Jima,
Rest forgotten, their shrieking, mortal hour
Transfigured to silence in the silent night.

Fireflies

The children race *now here* by the ivied fence,
gather squealing *now there* by the lily border.
The evening calms *the quickened air,* immense
and warm; its veil *is pierced with fire.* The order
of space discloses *as pair by pair* porch lights
carve shadows. *Cool phosphors flare* when dark
permits yearning *to signal where,* with spark
and pause and spark, *the fireflies are,* the sites
they spiral *when they aspire,* with carefree ardor
busy, *to embrace a star* that draws them thence.

Like children *we stand and stare,* watching the field
that twinkles *where gold wisps fare* to the end
of dusk, *as the sudden sphere,* ivory shield
aloft, *of moon stands clear* of the world's far bend.

Passage

The solemn pond displays the summer night
Perfect in the rondure of its speculum,
The sky set out in order, light by light.
Serenely *a muskrat noses through* the lines
Of stars; *the cool reflective moon* sways in
The water *that trembling languidly* but once
Now settles, *steadies itself again,* and shines
Impassive *within the astonished O,* again
Moveless, *upon the water's plane* immense.
Something has happened in the world this night
Of rare consequence for some time to come,
Whether or not it alters the final sum.

Development

a double sonnet

Negative

Camera made this woman a thing of mist
And shadow. Where she was dark the light now glows;
Where light, she softens from gray to gray, blonde rose
Charring, like a smoldering coal, to dust.
The cloudy lips that other lips have kissed
Smile with a secret they shall not disclose.
The eyes are burned to silver where time froze
And stare out from the irrepressible past.

Darkroom

Her ghost comes now to be baptized, to find
Within the acids, under the ruddy light,
Human aspect, site and circumstance,
The thing she is besides a thing of Mind,
What form becomes her in this transfiguring night,
What body embodies her to a world of chance
And ceaseless change, all-powerful and blind,
Where all things feel the sleepy grasp of blight.

Positive Print

And now that she is woman again, nuance
And form commingle to limn her image. Behind
This image, the ghost she was, the ghost she might
Become, surprises her appraising glance.
Her picture holds her spirit in its trance
And with the bright shapes dark, with dark the bright.

Janus

From east, from west the mirage caravans approach
the god with double face that guards *from west, from east* the gate of the lone citadel,
the garrison whose ruins here *attest, proclaim* that once it stood and things were well
within the deep-dug walls that now *proclaim, attest* the moldering force of time's grave touch.
    Along the narrow alleyways *the wind unwinds* its blind meander, troubles a patch
of alien grass. A swirl of dust *unwinds the wind* that spirals where the tower fell.
    The sun in its bronze chariot *arrives, departs*, without disturbing the spell
its stupor casts. The swift twilight *departs, arrives*; the night's close-huddled stars encroach
upon the sleepless sands. The gate with *double-single* god as sentry admits the moon
that with its marble gaze makes all things *single double*, as shadows slant from every ledge
and archivolt. Midnight, the moon has *moved unmoving* to the zenith and shines down
upon the double countenance, *unmoved, moving*, that stares out from the farthest ridge
of long horizon. Whatever event *it was, it is* again—as if transformed to stone—
that brought this place to desolation. *It is, it was*, it shall be here through every age.

Intruder

What can Little say of Big that Big needs said?
Why should Big take notice of the measly Small?

Entranced, I watch *the lucid drop*—like a silver ball
Displayed on baize—*that magnifies* the ivory thread
Within the surface, *the tiny vein* that shears across
The smooth velour *upon the leaf,* enclose the scene.
This little globe *reflects the skies* and draws within
Image of clouds *that steer the rain* to advance and pass,
Energies *to freshen life* this time again,
To round it off *and give it shape* in sphere-blown glass.

I am there too, spying, poking in my head,
Reflected, reflecting upon the All inside the All.

Once, Something, Never

It lingers beyond the threshold of recall,
an incident that was no incident,
a moment *something like a knothole* in a wall
of pine, *within the striate grain* an opening,
rupture *of the swift flow of days* which sped
unhalted, *that gave a placket glimpse* of happening
complete, *of one bright image that stamps,* even now
vivid, *with its moment of amaze.* It fled
at once, *its joy upon the brain* a glow
expired, *and the ever-yearning soul* has fed
upon what was only a presentiment
of something that was that never was at all.

Anecdote of the Ironweed

Shrunken and ragged, it leans slantwise to all
amid the jumble of the marshy, disused field
where touch-me-not, Budweiser cans, Joe Pye,
and gnarly tumble of honeysuckle vine,
of willow-clot and plastic grocery bags,
compound a jagged puzzle of the light,
background impure, all entangling with each—
the ironweed, never a single thing,
dies to manure the wilderness, the mess,
the industrious rot that feeds the moss and sludge
with mortal seed that mingles with other seed
to display a hardier sensibility
than that prissy, imperious jar in Tennessee.

Part Three

: in which the idea of the reliquary is developed. "A receptacle, such as a coffer or shrine, for keeping or displaying relics." In the Middle Ages relics were not only objects of veneration but economic resources as well. A church possessing the relic of a popular saint was insured of a faithful traffic of pilgrims who contributed to the well-being of the community.

The practice is widespread in its forms and venues. If you have kept a ticket stub from an Elvis concert in a drawer as a remembrance, the drawer has become a reliquary.

The first three of these poems are concerned with literal reliquaries.

The following six extend this figure in a conceit, the notion being that renowned literary relics (here, German Romantic poems in translation) are enclosed in new "reliquary" settings. The authors of the originals are identified.

"Pearl" uses the image of a casket for its jewel "of great price."

The Opulent Reliquary

Emerald, opal: A clutch of precious stone
Gleams on the breastplate, collar band, and crown;
The countenance is noble, calm, and stern
Of one in whom the fires of prophecy burn.

Look you: *Here lies the humerus* of John
The Baptist *in sumptuous estate,* arm-bone
Divine *of the shaggy evangelist* who lived
Apart, *an ascetic Nazarite,* and believed
In Christ, *who recognized Jesus* the Son
Of Man *in whom God was well pleased,* alone.

This reliquary was cast of silver and gold
In fourteenth-century Aachen. I am told
It hath performed many a miracle
For those who had lost faith or fallen ill.

Why then could it not prevent such harm
To him who lost his head before his arm?

The Re-Emended Reliquary

The structure of this silver countenance
Is known: *Inside the visage of gold* enchased
With gems *there stands a core of wood* to support
The mask, *enclosing the saintly skull,* all grin
And socket, *of the fulgent, haloed head* that once
Was that *of James, as we were told* this past
Decade *in the stately papal bull.* Report
Now comes it is St. Matthew's once again.

A Reliquary Letter

from Rome, year of our Lord 1403

Monsignor, I have made an inventory
Of relics found in Santa Maria Maggiore
In the wooden head of the Blessed Virgin Mary,
On the Coppo painting, that serves as reliquary:
The usual *knucklebones of saints* unknown;
Also, *from the Cross a nail,* the one
They say *that pierced our Savior's hand,* still bright;
Also, *the thimble that Mary wore* that night
So dread *when she sewed the tearful shroud* our Lord
Was laid in; *leaves from Gethsemane plants,* a hoard
Preserved, *enclosed in a crystal phial,* historied
And proud, *that a weary pilgrim found* half buried
In sand *upon a distant shore* one day
Years past *as he trudged that painful road* to pray.

Perhaps, Monsignor, it might be politic
To purchase these for your own bishopric.
Such objects help the faithful to keep faith
And each see envies what another hath
To advance the Father, Son, and Holy Ghost.
I say, we thieve—or buy at any cost.

Yours in the name of Jesus, Fra Fredric

A Conceit

This, the conceit: a fragment of Sappho is seen as a relic
    Precious and sacred to poets and lovers alike.
Through the millennia, scholars and critics have commented freely,
    Babbling with passions romantic, pedantic, and droll,
Heaping up footnotes, grammatical challenge in essays aggressive,
    Avid as silverfish feasting on raggedy scrolls.

Picture that massive volume of thought as costly container,
    Gold and enamel ornate with fine filigree,
Sappho's tense lines all nested within like bones of the saintly,
    Patient for worship by love-addled women and men.

Time disregards the reverend, brittle slivers of clavicle;
    Pilgrims adore the small reliquary of gold:
Scholars might hope that a like fate befall their eye-straining scribble—
    Sappho will shine through, even in limp paraphrase:

        Lucky, even godlike, seems to me he who,
        seated next to you, is listening, intent as
        your clear voice in peals of musical cadence
                        rings out merrily,

        sweetly laughing. Now my heart in my ribcage
        flutters; when I look at you for a moment
        I have lost the means to speak, and I swear that
                        quiet comes over me,

        tongue falls silent; skin glows warm with a burning
        flame; my eyes go sightless, dark as a starless
        night, a tintinabulum in my ears is
                        ringing to deafen me;

icy sweat suffuses me and a trembling
seizes me and pale I am as the grasses.
Death is near, I seem to feel its white presence
                    standing beside me . . .

Then in the personal stanza Catullus has added to Sappho,
    Weary lament recollects his Lesbian love:

Lassitude attacks Catullus, depression
clutches me, defeating all my endurance . . .
This is how they fell to ruin, those shining
                    cities and tall kings.

After such brilliance, poets but imitate, pouring out heatedly
    Ode after ode with their metaphors lifted from Sappho,
Passionate maybe but nothing original after Catullus,
    Nothing so vivid, nothing so plaintively brash.

Bring on the scholars and long may they furnish new textual
    Glosses, all adding baroque decoration with spades,
Burying the poem under a mountain of well-meaning, dull apparatus:
    Still will it flame out, its light a red ember of ice.

Pearl

Her hands were gentle about the ills of children,
Her speech was measured amid the quarrels of kinfolk.
She held *the sorrow that had grown* unspoken
Till it was *perfect as a sphere,* a token
Of her secret, *with a light that shone* within
And stood, *in an undropped tear,* a sign
Of what *enwrapped itself upon* the wound
Again, *layer on nacreous layer,* around
The hurt *till it transformed to stone,* mild jewel
Priceless, *modest, calm, and pure* and cool.

Here lies the lucent Pearl on black sateen
That shall not often enrobe her like again.

Doppelgängers

A man comes toward me out of the night,
Mumbling words I strain to hear.
At first he seems bereft of sight,
So empty and so fixed his stare.

Closer he draws into the deep
Shadow cast by the gambrel roof,
Then halts. The city lies asleep
As he and I stand stiff, aloof.

The hour is mine. He must break
The silence, be the one to tell
The sorrows that goad him here to speak
To me as I stand sentinel.

  The night is still, the streets deserted;
  In this house once lived my beloved.
  This town she long ago departed;
  The house yet stands in place unmoved.

  A man stands here. He stares into space
  And clenches his hands in agony
  And when I look into his face
  It is my moonlit self I see:

  My Double. "O pale Companion,
  Why post you here under the moon,
  Aping the tortures that were mine
  So many times, in time now gone?"

Since we were not created whole
But were two always, you and I,
She must have feared our bisected soul—
So I might say. But make no reply.

—Heinrich Heine, "Der Doppelgänger"

On an Antique Picture

We sat smoking when the orders came,
But we marched out, exhausted, lame,
Over the caisson-littered road.
Winkler turned to me and said:

> *Look there in the flowering glade,*
> *Its pond all veiled with catkin reed,*
> *How that innocent little chap*
> *Gambols in the Virgin's lap,*
> *While in the forest just across*
> *Green grows the tree to make his cross.*

That was not Mary and her child.
Corporal Winkler had been beguiled
By the famous painting in the town
We left after we burnt it down.

—Eduard Mörike, "Auf ein Altes Bild"

Receptionist

Herr Belden is in conference.
Please take the seat there by the door.
Herr Bloch is on the train to France.
Fräulein Froh is on line four.

> *I'll lay me down in the dark grove;*
> *The trees shall murmur over me*
> *And the deep night that arches above*
> *With its cloak of stars shall cover me.*

Please take the seat there by the door.
Herr Bestermann will see you soon.
Frau Weisensach is on line four.
Herr Seitz can meet with you at noon.

> *The little brook shall come to inquire*
> *If I am sleeping safe and tight,*
> *But I shall keep awake to hear*
> *The nightingales sing through the night.*

Herr Biedermann should see you soon.
His conference is running late.
Herr Seitz will meet with you at noon.
The tax reports come in at eight.

> *And the treetops will sway and moan,*
> *Soughing the whole night through . . .*
> *—These thoughts come to me alone,*
> *Singing what none else can know.*

It seems, Herr Schmidt, they're running late.
Herr Ritter passed away long since.
Those tax reports were due at eight.
Herr Belden's still in conference.

—Joseph von Eichendorff, "Die Einsame"

On Louise's Burning Her Faithless Lover's Letters; or, Sympathetic Magic

"Conceived in love's dark melancholy,
then to the faithless world delivered,
now from those times you are dissevered—
so burn, my children of heartsick folly!"

> *Some part of me I cannot name*
> *is disappearing like thin smoke*
> *drifting over field and brook:*
> *some part of me devoured by flame.*

"From flame of Eros you were born,
and now to flame are borne again:
For never for me alone his pen
set down those words I hold in scorn."

> *Some part of me does not exist,*
> *some part of me already gone,*
> *as when the furious noonday sun*
> *burns away a morning mist.*

"And now you burn. And now depart.
No trace of you will here remain.
But he who sent you . . . Ah! That man
still may glimmer within my heart."

> *Am I a being purified*
> *as by a transformative fire*
> *of feeling stronger than desire?*
> *Do I yet live? Or have I died?*

—Gabriele von Baumberg, "Als Luise die Briefe . . ."

The Listeners

By forest edge we heard their words,
Maiden and Death in dialogue.
The oaks were thick with silent birds
And from the moss rose a thin fog.

Maiden

Go by, go by!
Bony Man, leave me alone.
I am too young to die.
Touch me not, Belovèd One.

Death

Give me your slender hand, my sweet.
I come as friend to you in peace
And do not wish to cause you fright.
In my arms you shall sleep at ease.

She was a lovely, gentle thing.
Her lover had fallen in the war.
This night the birds would never sing.
We had heard such talk before.

—Matthias Claudius, "Der Tod und das Mädchen"

Part Four

: *Counterpoint:* in which this musical term, meaning two or more lines that sound simultaneously, independently, and interdependently, applies to describe a single unified effect. J. S. Bach's two-part inventions provide a handy analogy.

In the following pieces, a debate or dialectic is established between the two "melodic" lines, but these dissensions or complementaries are designed to produce a final harmony.

Shadow Box

Corpus.   *Spiritus.*

1

Sad Flesh, you are no more *than what a candle is,*
    Its corporal presence, now wasting by flame *each hour,*
As the soul-wick within the core *gives in to fire,*
    Leaps upward, melting to vapor *that strays*
Along air currents dark and impure, *twisted and dour*
And flimsy as words on paper, *the nobler you aspire.*

2

    Poor Ghost, *you are no more* than guess
Of priest and sage, no more *than nothingness* dressed out
In cobweb rhetoric, *wherein the mind* in doubt
To calm itself *must try to find* its nakedness
    A mortal *sheltering for* a time so brief
    On earth *its grave distress* is its whole life.

Unknowing

We know that what we do not know will be
    greater always than what we know,
concealed within the physic of the sea,
    the stone, the star, the faceless snow,
powers that intimidate humanity,
    extend domains to which we bow.

As when a forest opens onto sky
    where clouds voyage their blue kingdom
and we see insubstantial alps scroll by,
    massively weightless, eloquent, dumb,
to challenge the rude judgment of the eye,
    there we heap thoughts we cannot plumb;

or as the mother hears her children play,
    chanting in the Maytime yard,
and sees from her screened window with a sigh
    bright creatures of a time unmarred,
unnerving images of a long-ago day,
    foreshadow all that Mother feared:

so tidings of a universe unknown,
    unknowable ever to the mind,
murmur to us from an uncharted zone,
    the world before us and behind,
wherein we stand apart but not alone—
    seek not, if you would find.

Second Law

If the universe expands, why do I feel
so drained, as if *a pinprick somewhere* goes psss
and slowly *loses the air,* with an adder hiss
unmusical, *out of a hole* that will not seal
while time runs on, *into a whole* outside
our own *the savants fear* and sometimes deride?
Some say it *may not be there,* only as real
as the next charming theory may decide.

Music Box

"I weary of country music," says Madeline,
"The hangdog sentiment and dobro whine.
Too frequent and *too sad that song* of love
In smithereens, *the same old tune* whereof
They always howl. *'She Done Me Wrong'* we know
By heart, as sung *again and again*, oh woe
Dependable *as moon and sun*. Their thoughts
Tend ever to *come round in a ring*, like boats
In dazed maelstroms, *like rondo refrain* gone mad.
No more of that. *Best to sing none*," she said.
"Wolfgang Amadeus suits me just fine.
À bas that hillbilly crap," cried Madeline.

Bachsmusik

"His concertos make me dizzy," said Hermann Broch,
"And all those dense chaconnes of J. S. Bach.
I feel *the lines crisscross* and then they go
Apart; *and then crosscriss* till vertigo
Ensues, and then *the notes will pass* each other
Like swifts in flight *and now repass* another
Time and place *and tightly weave*, disjoin,
Return again *and interweave*, in line
On line on line, *like cresting wave* advancing
Beachward to crowd *on tumbling wave*, all dancing,
Leaping, retreating, surging forward, back,
Until I feel quite ill," said Hermann Broch.

Friendship

She.   *He.*

Friendship may be a passion too,
   Say the sages, gray and cold,
   When all the youthful story's told,
As may be seen in me and you;
Our days are pleasant, wild nights few;
   A new arrangement must unfold
   As silver hair replaces gold,
And I to you at last prove true
And I to you at last prove true.

Discretion

She.   He.

I have heard them say some things you said
Of us when we were foolish young;
  Untrue or true, those ancient tales
  Of love when all our days were spring
  Inspire remembrance as passion fails
  And the sunrise lark forbears to sing—
But I would have you stop your tongue
And keep your silence till I am dead.

Secrets

She.   *He.*

I know that you withhold from me
Secrets I would not like to hear,
    Suspicions, petty fears and hates,
    Humiliations, small defeats,
    Gossip unfounded or on the mark,
    Piddling disgraces best kept dark—
But does not perfect honesty
Make these the things you should declare?
    I only keep from you those shames
    So drab I cannot give them names.

Revolution and Permanence

Sea.   *Waves.*

A dream perturbs my mind:

> *Somewhere far a wind*
> *Pummels the peaceful main*
> *Till its whole being grinds*
> *And grain by gleaming grain*
> *I construct the land—*

That storm shall in me find
Fierce creatures that live unseen
To thrust upon the sand.

We bring, we take away:
That shall to you return,
Your children of the deep;
> When the planet lies asleep,
> And the sun no longer shall burn
> Nor night turn into day
> Then I reclaim my own
As mountains and deserts drown.

Duties

Sleep.   *Dream.*

Each night I host the bright parade,
    Vivid phantoms who come to tell
Of tenuous omens happy or sad,
    Tales of things that never befell,
That trouble the pilgrim's restless bed,
    Visions of paradise and of hell.

Without dark Sleep Dream could not be,
    Without bright Dream Sleep is but death
    Wherein the body continues to breathe,
And human life a falsity.

Process

Secret

And now *it is a clench of ice* quartz-hard,
center *round which the soul collects,* shivering
in pain, *and self-delusion protects* as best
it can *with untrue memories* years-thick.

Listen: *It is the voice that says,* midnight,
noontide, *the truth is in you still;* you know
its weight, *no matter what you will,* burden
to bear *till the end of all your days* on earth.

Confession

Confess: The secret that tears your sleep, *shackles
your spirit,* and seals within itself, *as in
a vault,* its self-destroying proof, *denied
so often,* is one you cannot keep *or silence.*

Admit: The secret possesses you *body
and soul* as a servile property; *it grips
you close* and will not set you free *or loosen
its hold,* no matter what you do *or say.*

Absolution

Forgive *the secret that has eaten* your substance,
murdered *the person that you were,* so that
your hope *is made to disappear* almost
entire, *like chalk to powder beaten,* windblown.

Forget: *It has not buried your life,* devoted
to defend *that which you most lived for;* it struck
and yet *it could not break the core* credo;
the tenets *of your heartfelt belief* still stand.

Duologue

Spirit.   *Mind.*

Buried in logic, what can you find,
   Shackled to flesh, what can you see
About the madcap world beyond.
   Of Time's wild timeless mystery?

Chained to reason, do you believe,
   Prey of passion, can you analyze
What five blunt senses cannot perceive,
   What lawless prospect before you lies?

You, false sister, must fare purblind,
   You, dear sister, first spoke my name.
   O, great mother, lend me your flame!
O, lost daughter, hold me in mind!

Counterpoint

Stone.   *Water.*

1

I have attested all that I may be:
> *but all that I may be is yet to know;*
what you find in me is as you see;
> *thwarted, I find out strange ways to flow;*
here stand I image of eternity;
> *where once I was I am never now.*

2

My surface recreates the land and sky;
> who mirrors not, that being is content;
I show things moving yet they pass not by;
> and I am I and need no other consent;
I change and change but hold my identity;
> I keep my strength when all beside is spent.

Nocturnal

Cat.   Dog.

These rooms now I patrol
While every other soul
  Lies in the depths of sleep;
And in the frosty yard
I stand vigilant guard
  And all the border keep.

Chorus

Dream, masters of the day;
Under the twinkling sky
 We hold you safe and sound
As the perilous hours roll by
And you mutter, snore, and sigh
 In bourgeois oblivion drowned.

Duet

Author.   *Book.*

Go, little flustered one, and tell
    what things there are beneath, beyond
us beings whose timid senses fail
    the world that lies on every hand,
our aspirations shall not quail,
    our destinies shall not confound.

A steely wisdom I impart,
    though it be only poetry,
confected with laborious art,
    for those who have the means to see,
it carries sharp into the heart,
    it lodges there until they die.

Part Five

: in which ancient Christian Latin hymns provide context and subject matter. A Latin stanza is quoted and its syllables disposed in order throughout the English-language stanzas of commentary and elaboration. A translation of the Latin closes each poem.

Any Western language we choose to speak and read enfolds the prayers of our past ages.

Two Latin Hymns

I

Veni, creator Spiritus,
Mentes tuorum visita:
Imple superna gratia
Quae tu creasti pectora.

To venial men may come an unsought hour
Of peaceful joy—as when an acre of clay
Cratered and torn by war, new-fallen snow,
With the spirit of sleep and its cool power,
Prepares for happier use—to soothe the day
That follows like a beneficent amen;
Its slow, silent estuarial flow
The mind may misperceive, or may deny,
Self-prisoned in an umbra where terrors lour.

And yet, a visitation of such relief
Shall implement the possibility
That sweet, supernal grace may come again
To calm the violent motion of a sharp grief,
To quell a rising fury, and quieten
The pangs a mean, unlucky reality
Instills in the peccable soul.

Grant us belief,
O Lord Protector, amend the losel life.

Come, fecundive Ghost,
Visit this worldly host,
Flood with supernal grace
Us, Your created race.

Accende lumen sensibus,
Infunde amorem cordibus,
Infirma nostri corporis,
Virtute firmans perpeti.

Accepting that we cannot know our ends,
Elusive, immense as the insensible verges
Of the sky, we busy our swift days
In fungible pursuits, so one hour blends
With an indefinable next, mist and haze
Mutually embracing: Thus, amorous urges
Flare up and sink to embers as time emends
And cordial mistrust darkens the fond gaze;
Thus, the bustling of our infirmities
Defers all manly resolution, delays
Purposeful action; pleasures transform to scourges,
Delights to trials. Fear corrupts and rends
The spirit; where valiance was, gray torpor is.

Virtue, Lord, with your tutelary grace
Make firm in us, that we may answer to
Asperity, and lend us strength to face
Our defiled future: Thus we petition You.

Light to our senses give;
Into our hearts bring love;
To our frail weaknesses
Supply firm steadiness.

Per te sciamus da Patrem.
Nosciamus atque Filium.
Te utriusque Spiritum
Credamus omni tempore.

Perpend, Eternal Sire, on this Thy grace;
Illumine our dour nescience with grace:

Forgive the sullen, willful ignoramus;
Forgive the smug, the damfool, and the shameless,
The thug, the cruel and manic patriotic,
The snitch, the trembling, self-deceived neurotic,
The seeker after nostrums, the tainted juror,
The mountebank and scamming usurer,
The hatred-monger, the quester after gurus,
The fixer, liar, the humbug with a screw loose.

Tear from our hearts the uttermost deep shame
And feed in us the ardor of our flame;
Query the spirit of Humanity
And reason it from incredulity;
Damn us, if so the golden scales demand
(Though You in all omniscience understand),
Or temper us in the refining fire
And forge us trusty steel, Eternal Sire.

Through You the Father is known,
Through You is known the Son.
Grant that we comprehend
How You from them descend.

II

Te lucis ante terminum
Rerum creator poscimus
Ut solita clementia
Sis praesul ad custodiam

Tell us, as we watch the sun decline,
How lucent is the darkness You have spared;
Anterior to Your all-pervasive light,
It stands as terminus and origin;
Before all number was, before Your Word
Was spoken to be read by human sight
In nature, and in the rumble of its working heard,
There hid You, Creator Father, in that night
Potent, sciential, and as yet unstarred,
Musing the lineaments of Your design.

Shut down our striving for the Absolute,
Acquit us of the duty to imitate
With our small deeds Your austere clemency;
Sow in us devotion to defeat;
Urge us resistant to Your charity;
Take from us our long praenominal pride
And let us sully ourselves with foul deceit—
We still, O Lord, are Your sad flock the same,
Still we shelter in Your kind custody;
And when You query, each still responds, "I am!"

With your accustomed clemency,
Creator of all things that are,
Before the sun departs the sky,
We pray You keep us in Your care.

Procul recedant somnia
Et noctium phantasmata
Hostemque nostrum comprime
Ne polluantur corpora.

When the lonely night proposes
Brash temptations that culminate
In angry climax then recede,
Still defiant and irate,
It to the insomniac discloses
A yet unspoken, hungry need.

Nocturnal remorse crowds round to pour
Sweaty delirium over him;
Familiar phantasms return once more,
Whining, tattered, insolent, grim;
A host of spectral accusers demand
Empathies he cannot profess
And their bleak sequent judgments stand
Noxious in their just redress;
A strumpet image appears in guise
Of Love once lost to compromise;
A taloned Fury in sharp silhouette
Advances, by moonlight ill met.

At last the ghost-negating dawn
Brings to the man a politic
Ablution. As the hours wear on
Scant traces of the long hysteric
Nighttime return in awkward spates
The lonely day incorporates.

When at night our beds we keep,
Protect our dreams and keep them free;
Let the Foe not vex our sleep
With polluting fantasy.

Praesta, Pater Omnipotens,
Per Jesum Christum Dominum,
Qui tecum in perpetuum
Regnat cum Sancto Spirito.

Father All-Powerful, we pray that You
Establish now forever a timeless Law
That spares no one its mercy, no thing its due;
Us Your people consternate with awe
As we discover love omnipotent
Tensing the mechanic universe
To harmonies perpetually unspent.
With Jesus guide us through the daily course
That must not be the sum of what we are;
With Your Christ steady us in the shattered plain
Where bloody tumult of the zealous war
Dominates the will with tearing pain
And devout numbers rise to fall again.
Quieten the fears that accumulate
In all offenses that we perpetrate
And lead Your petulant children from cold pride
To the humbling, enheartening fireside.

Regnant Father, attend us as we fare
Toward the night of our viaticum;
Sanction the passions that within us loom;
O Founder Spirit, use us all each hour.

Support us, Father Omnipotent,
With Christ Jesus stand our friend
And with the Holy Ghost benevolent
From all Beginning to the End.

afterword

Loe here are wonders, we have more Poets than judges and interpreters of poesie. It is an easier matter to frame it, than to know it: But the good and loftie, the supreme and divine, is beyond rules, and above reason.

> —Montaigne, *Essays,* bk. I, chap. XXXVI, "Of Cato the Younger"